Russian Tortoises in Captivity

Jerry D. Fife

Professional Breeders Series®

E C O

© 2012 by ECO Herpetological Publishing & Distribution.

Printed in China

ISBN 978-0-9788979-8-7

Copies available from:

ECO Herpetological Publishing & Distribution
P. O. Box 376 Rodeo, NM 88056 USA
telephone: 575-557-5757   fax: 575-557-7575
email: ecoorders@hotmail.com   website: http://www.reptileshirts.com

LIVING ART publishing   Zoo Book Sales
http://www.livingartpublishing.com   http://www.zoobooksales.com

Design and layout by Russ Gurley.
Cover design by Chad DeBoard.

Front Cover: An adult Russian tortoise by Jerry Fife.
Back Cover: A hatching tortoise by Jerry Fife.

ACKNOWLEDGEMENTS

Thanks to those who supplied animals or photos for this project, including Russ Gurley, Amanda Ebenhack, Phil Goss, Bill Love, Drew Rheinhardt, Linda Putnam, Jeff and Kim Gee, Torsten Blanck, Jim Barzyk, Betty Kent, Jan Ševík, Chris Rosher, Jeff Littlejohn Wolfgang Wegehaupt, Mark and Kim Bell, and Richard Fife.

TABLE OF CONTENTS

INTRODUCTION

An adult female Russian tortoise emerging from hibernation in her outdoor enclosure. Photo by Jerry Fife.

The tortoises of the Mediterranean and Eurasia include five groups: Greek tortoises, Hermann's tortoises, Marginated tortoises, Russian tortoises, and Egyptian tortoises. This book will discuss the captive care and breeding of Russian tortoises, but the care of most of the Mediterranean species is very similar.

Russian tortoises have a long history in the pet trade and have been exported to the United States, Europe, and Asia for many years. In fact, Russian tortoises continue to be among the most common species imported into the United States. From 1976 to 1993, over one million (1,097,300) Russian tortoises were reportedly collected and traded in Kazakhstan. It is hard to imagine that any tortoise species could withstand this level of collection without a negative impact to native populations.

A carapace and plastron view of hatchling Russian tortoises. The other Mediterranean species lack the entirely black plastron of the Russian hatchling. Photo by Jerry Fife.

Some countries have taken action to protect their native populations of Mediterranean tortoises (Spain, Italy, France, and Greece), but trade continues from other countries. All *Testudo* species, other than *T. kleinmanni* which is Appendix I, are now protected by Appendix II of C.I.T.E.S. (Convention on Trade in Endangered Flora and Fauna). Of course, protection does not mean that trade is forbidden or illegal, it only means that it is monitored with paperwork. Thankfully, tortoise keepers in the United States and Europe are breeding Russian tortoises in increasing numbers and captive-hatched specimens are now commonly available.

This book will provide information on the care of these popular tortoises, which will allow hobbyists to be successful in maintaining their tortoises and most importantly, to encourage captive breeding to hopefully remove the need to collect wild specimens.

The systematics and taxonomy of tortoises is constantly under review and debate. The genus *Testudo*, which has traditionally included Greek tortoises, Hermann's tortoises, Marginated tortoises, and Egyptian tortoises, in addition to Rusian tortoises, is perhaps

Adult Russian tortoises that have recently been imported into the United States.

experiencing the most revisions and reclassifications of any other group of tortoises. Each of the five forms have been separated into a number of subspecies and there are some subspecies which have recently been elevated to species status. Hermann's tortoises have been classified by some taxonomists as *Eurotestudo* and Egyptian tortoises were proposed for a new genus, *Pseudotestudo*, but both of these moves seem to be invalid or at least not accepted by many tortoise specialists so far. The Russian tortoises have been moved out of the genus *Testudo* to the genus *Agrionemys*.

Original Description: Gray, J.E. 1844. Catalogue of Tortoises, Crocodilians, and Amphisbaenians in the Collection of the British Museum. British Museum (Natural History), London. viii + 80 p.

Currently, there are four recognized species (or subspecies) of Russian tortoises.

Agrionemys horsfieldii GRAY 1844 or *Testudo horsfieldii horsfieldii*. (Northern Central Asia)

Agrionemys kazachstanica Chkhikvadze, 1988 or *Testudo horsefieldii kazachtanica*. (Southern Central Asia)

Agrionemys rustamovi Chkhikvadze, Amirashvili & Ataev, 1990 or *Testudo horsefieldii rustmovi*. (Southern Turkmenia)

Agrionemys baluchiorum Annandal, 1906 (Southeastern Iran and southwestern Pakistan)

These may in the future be separated again. The identification of the different species by external characters only is not easy.

A. rustamovi has a low shell but regularly convex, the bridge is slightly elevated at the margins, and has a brown-fawn general background color.

A. horsfieldii has a higher, regularly arched, rounded shell, the bridge elevated at the margins, a round border of the shell, and the background is brown with large, blurred, darker blotches.

A. kazachstanica has a low depressed shell, sometimes very flat, with a border more or less enlarged in the rear, the bridge is elevated at the margin; the background color is brown-yellowish to yellowgreenish with blackish blotches of various sizes but with well-defined borders on each scute.

Russian Tortoises in Nature

Russian tortoises have a huge range in nature, living from Iran in the west to China in the east, Russia in the north, and the Gulf of Oman and Pakistan in the south. This tortoise was previously (and still is by some) included within the genus *Testudo*. It is currently

A group of Russian tortoises showing the variety of specimens that have arrived in importations to the United States. Photo by Phil Goss.

included in the genus *Agrionemys* by most tortoise researchers. The members of this genus include tortoises specialized for burrowing and adapted for extremely severe climates (Lagarde, 2004). There are drastic differences in the burrowing activities of these tortoises and they are likely to be separated into individual species the future (Guyot-Jackson, pers. com.).

In nature, most Russian tortoises will excavate long burrows in which to hide and avoid extreme temperatures, though some populations burrow much less than others. Russian tortoises are rather flat and round in shape. The color may vary but is generally a greenish brown coloration. There are also some tan and black specimens.

This species is also called by the common name of the "Four-toed tortoise" as it only has four claws on the forelimbs, in contrast to members of the genus *Testudo* which have five. Some Hermann's tortoises may appear to have four toes, however their skeleton shows five.

The largest specimens of *A. horsfieldii* reach 11 inches (28 cm), while *A. kazachstanica* do not exceed 8 inches (20 cm). *A. kazachs-*

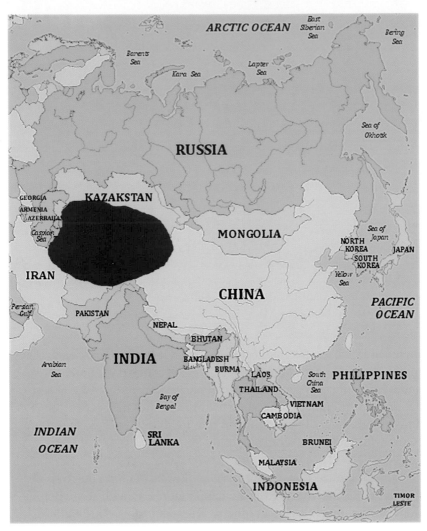

The range of *A. horsfieldii* in nature.

tanica is the most common species of Russian tortoise imported into the United States.

Due to their extensive range, Russian tortoises experience a wide range of habitats, however they are generally found in dry steppes and desert habitats at altitudes up to 8,200 feet (2,500 meters) with very hot summers and severe winters as experienced in Russia and the Black Sea area. They are also found near springs and brooks where grasses and other vegetation are relatively abundant.

Agrionemys h. kazachstanica, habitat in Kazakhstan.

Russian tortoises will feed on herbaceous and succulent vegetation, including grasses, fresh leaves, flowers, fruit, and supple twigs and stems of native plants. During a rainstorm, the tortoise may drink from puddles which form. It will usually pass urine at this time. Uric acid, which appears as white paste, is often passed by tortoises following rain when water is available for replenishment. Though they live in arid habitats they spend much of their time in burrows which have higher humidity levels.

In nature, due to harsh weather conditions, their active period may only last three or four months in parts of their range. During this period of activity the tortoises eat and grow fast, gaining significant weight. According to researchers, the males of *A. horsfieldii* have an energy output higher than that of any other reptile, to take maximum advantage of the four months activity cycle (Bonin, Devaux, Dupre, 2006).

The onset of high summer temperatures causes the tortoises to retreat to their burrows to estivate in June, July, and August. This is soon followed by a move toward hibernation in October to February.

Female Russian tortoises grow larger than males and have shorter tails. Both sexes have a flat carapace and a flat plastron. Males do

A typical imported adult Russian tortoise. Photo by Jerry Fife.

not exhibit the concave plastrons seen in many male tortoises. Males grow to approximately 6 inches (15 cm) and females can grow to 8 inches (20 cm).

Females lay 2-6 eggs and may lay two or three clutches beginning in April or May. The eggs incubate for 80 to 110 days with hatchlings emerging in August or September. In nature (and outdoor enclosures in captivity), the hatchlings may overwinter in the nest and emerge the following spring.

Chapter ONE: Russian Tortoises In Captivity

There are many factors which must be considered when choosing a tortoise.

To determine what species is best for you will depend on your circumstances. For example, do you live in a cold or warm climate? Do you live in a humid or arid climate? Do you have space for a large tortoise or only a small tortoise? Do you have space to keep the tortoise outside or only inside? How much are you willing to spend on the tortoise and its care and maintenance?

A very large adult Russian tortoise. This is the maximum size this species typically attains. Photo by Phil Goss.

Which Species is Best for You?

To determine which species is best for you will depend on your answers to the previous questions and the questions to follow. Each species has different requirements. An African Spurred tortoise may look cute as a two inch hatchling but do you have space for a 100

A pair of Russian tortoises exploring their outdoor enclosure. Photo by Jerry Fife.

pound tortoise in your house if it can't be outside during the winter in your area? A smaller Russian or Hermann's tortoise may be a better choice if it needs to be kept indoors, however maybe you don't want to deal with hibernation. Specific research on the size, climate and personality of tortoises will help you determine what species is best for you.

What are your goals? Do you just want a pet? Do you want to keep multiple tortoises or multiple species? Do you want to breed the tortoise? Do you want a tortoise that is active year round or is it OK if it hibernates or is inactive a large portion of the year? Some tortoise species are very secretive and shy away from interaction with people, while others seem to enjoy the presence of their owner.

While we may understand these issues, many people still purchase a tortoise based on impulse, availability, or price. Many people want the prettiest tortoise or perhaps the cheapest tortoise for their child. Buying a tortoise because it is cute or because it is cheap, without understanding the requirements for its care will results in a high degree or mortality. Most cheap tortoises are recent imports, which often require a trip to a veterinarian who specializes in reptiles. If the owner purchased the tortoise because it is cheap, they likely will not be willing to spend the money to treat it for parasites. It is often cheaper to pay more for a captive-hatched tortoise, than to pay the cost of a wild import and related veterinary costs.

People that purchase a "cute little" tortoise may be disappointed to learn that it is a species which will become too large for them to house when it grows to an adult.

A tortoise is a long-term commitment. They live much longer than most pets and a hatchling must be purchased with the understanding of how large it will grow, housing requirements, diet, and care requirements over its entire life. The owner must understand the responsibilities and commitment associated with their acquisition.

Russian tortoises and other Mediterranean species are popular pet tortoises for several reasons.

1. Availability - Russian species are commonly imported and have recently been captive-bred. Russian tortoises are becoming more commonly available at many pet shops.

2. Price - The high number of imports keeps prices low. Imports typically are less expensive than captive-hatched specimens.

3. Size - Unlike African Spurred tortoises and Leopard tortoises which grow large, Russian tortoises are relatively small. The Russian tortoise is smaller than most pet species and therefore easier to house indoors than African Spurred or Leopard tortoises.

4. Personality - Russian tortoises have an outgoing personality. Even wild-caught specimens will quickly learn to come to their owner for food.

5. Temperature range - Russian tortoises can tolerate a wide range of temperatures and therefore can be kept outdoors year round in many areas where other species would require artificial heat. However be aware that Russian tortoises do not generally do well with high humidity.

Though cute, and wide-eyed, this African spurred tortoise will soon grow quite large and beyond what many pet keepers are able to accomodate. Photo by Russ Gurley.

The reasons Russian tortoises may **not** be the best choice include:

1. Housing - Often males and females must be kept separated due to aggression during breeding season. If you want to keep multiple males and females together, another species such as Leopards or Star tortoises may be better.

2. Hibernation - Russian tortoises will hibernate in the wild. If you want a tortoise that is active year round, be sure to choose a species that doesn't hibernate such as Redfoots, Yellowfoots, African Spurred, or Star tortoises.

3. Digging - Russian tortoises may dig long, horizontal burrows and each of the species enjoy digging into the substrate or the ground of their enclosures. This digging is however minimal compared to the African Spurred tortoise.

4. Color - Though some species are quite colorful, some people have

expressed that Russians (and the other Mediterranean tortoises) are not as pretty as other species of tortoises.

5. Escape Artists - Russian, Hermann's, and some of the Greeks are great escape artists. Perhaps only the Pancake tortoises is a better climber. In addition to being great climbers, they will wedge themselves in a corner to climb out of an enclosure. Even many experienced keepers have had one of these species find their way out of their enclosures.

Wild-Caught Tortoises

Though not all the Mediterranean tortoises are still imported into the United States, Russians tortoises are still imported. Western Hermann's tortoises and Marginated tortoises are protected throughout their range and are no longer exported. Egyptian tortoises are listed on Appendix I of C.I.T.E.S. and are no longer imported.

Generally, wild-caught, imported tortoises are cheaper to purchase than captive-hatched tortoises. They often appear to be perfect specimens; however appearances are often not what they seem. Wild-caught specimens may have a difficult time acclimating to captive conditions and generally harbor parasites or may have diseases. Often the stress of importation and crowded conditions may cause increased parasite loads or expose healthy tortoises to sick and diseased animals.

Older specimens can have a very difficult time adjusting to captivity after having lived in the wild for several decades.

Many people have learned that purchasing a cheap wild-caught import actually costs more than a more expensive captive-bred tortoise, once veterinary costs are included. Other people simply end up with a dead tortoise and conclude that tortoises are too difficult to maintain. This is unfortunately the fate of many imported tortoises in the pet industry. This, however, is changing as shipping standards have improved and the husbandry of tortoises is better understood.

Wild-caught imported tortoises should be examined by a qualified reptile veterinarian and treated appropriately. Once treated, an acclimated imported tortoise will usually do well. Some species seem to handle importation better than others and some, such as Hinge-backed tortoises, Impressed tortoises, and others should not be purchased by beginning keepers as imported specimens have a very high mortality rate.

Purchasing A Tortoise

Once you have determined that a Russian tortoise is the best tortoise for you, the next question is, where do I get it?

There are three main alternatives:

1. Pet Shop,
2. Reptile Show or Expo,
3. Direct from the breeder

Pet Shops

Pet shops are increasingly offering non-traditional pets. Some shops specialize in reptiles and offer tortoises and all the supplies necessary for their care and maintenance. Few pet shops will regularly carry many species of tortoise. Most common in the United States are captive-hatched African Spurred tortoises and whatever species is currently being imported. Russian tortoises are commonly imported and most of the large chain stores regularly have at least one species available. Pet shop employees may have limited knowledge on their care and maintenance but should be able to direct you to the latest products available and basic care requirements.

Many general pet shops in the United States just offer inexpensive reptiles and may not carry any tortoises. If they do have tortoises they are generally wild-caught imports such as Russian, Redfoots, or Hinge-back tortoises and perhaps captive-bred African Spurred tortoises.

At the store, check the tortoise enclosures, if the tortoises are over crowded, if they mix multiple species, feed an incorrect diet, do not provide adequate light or heat, avoid purchasing a tortoise from these establishments.

Inquire at the pet store if they offer veterinary services for the tortoises and what, if any, guarantee is provided. While a store cannot control how you keep the tortoise, a healthy tortoise should easily survive several weeks in less than optimal conditions, therefore a one week guarantee is reasonable.

Key factors to consider and look for in the selection of a tortoise include:

· The tortoise should be alert, strong, and heavy (Select a strong, heavy tortoise.)

· It should have a hard, firm shell (If the shell is "mushy" it should be avoided.)

· It should have clear eyes and nose (Clear and free from bubbles or discharge.)

· It should have a clear, clean vent. (Runny stools stain the vent and may be an indication of parasites or poor diet; however it may also just be the result of a diet high in store-bought greens.)

· The shell should be free of damage. (This may be just cosmetic, assuming the shell has healed. Greek tortoises and Russian tortoises are often imported with damaged but healed shells.)

· Is the tortoise a wild-caught, imported, or long-term captive or captive-hatched? (Ask about the origin of the tortoise. Captive-hatched or long-term captives generally have less health issues and are more used to the food you will provide and are more used to human contact.)

Reptile Shows and Expos

Reptile shows have become increasingly common across the United States and may offer you a chance to see a large selection and variety of tortoises. They generally have captive-bred animals

A crowd of reptile hobbyists at the North American Reptile Breeders Conference, USA. Photo by Bill Love.

and often breeders display and sell their own hatchlings. The overall health, quality and quantity of tortoises available often exceed that of pet shops. Many reptile shows will include Russian, Hermann's, Greeks and Marginated tortoises; however Egyptian and some of the rarer Mediterranean species are not common. The reptile expo provides the buyer an opportunity to ask questions and examine a larger selection of tortoises and hand pick the specimen they prefer. Personal preference in color, size, and other characteristics by comparing multiple tortoises is a major advantage in purchasing a tortoise at a reptile expo. These shows generally offer cheaper prices than pet stores and eliminate shipping costs of purchases from an out-of-state breeder or over the Internet.

The main disadvantage of buying at a reptile show is that many of the vendors are not local and follow-up if there are any concerns with your purchase may be more difficult than dealing with your local pet store. Many vendors return to the shows each year or several times a year and will provide phone or email assistance, however the possibility exists that the vendor may not accurately represent the tortoises. Some vendors may attempt to sell imported animals as long-term captives or captive-hatched.

The author, Jerry Fife, at his booth at the Anaheim NARBC show. Photo by Drew Rheinhardt.

It is important to ask about the origin of the tortoise and other questions to evaluate if the vendor is knowledgeable and truthfully representing the tortoise. Remember, if the deal seems too good to be true, it probably is!

A wild-caught specimen should be less expensive than a captive-hatched specimen. Always make sure the tortoise feels heavy and has clear eyes and nostrils. A tortoise can be easily treated for parasites, however if it is underweight and appears sick, it may require expensive veterinary care, a significant time commitment, including tube feeding, etc. It may also carry a virus or disease which could spread to other tortoises in your collection. Buying a sick tortoise to save it is best left to very experienced rehabbers and those with veterinary skills.

There are many excellent reptile shows across the country. The dates and locations of these shows can be found on the Internet, *REPTILES* magazine (or Reptile Channel.com), or through a local herpetological association.

A very unusual occurence. These conjoined Russian tortoises were produced by a private breeder. Photo by Russ Gurley. Courtesy of Betty Kent.

Tortoise Breeders

The best place to purchase a tortoise is directly from the breeder. Breeders will have a better understanding of how to care for the tortoise and can explain how to best maintain your tortoise. They should be able to answer each of your questions and provide detailed help on set-up, diet, and breeding of your tortoise. If you meet a local breeder, this eliminates the cost and stress of shipping. While some breeders prefer to only sell wholesale, most will sell individual tortoises. Some breeders may allow you to visit their facility which can provide great insight into housing and care. If the breeder is in your area, you can find out if the tortoise can be hibernated naturally, how they protect their tortoises from predators, and much more. By examining the adult tortoises you will have a good idea what your tortoise will look like as it matures. The breeder should know the bloodline and can ensure unrelated tortoises if your goal is captive breeding. Tortoise breeders can be found at reptile expos, through the Internet, or at local reptile clubs. References are always desirable.

Buyer Beware

The purchase of any live animal involves some risk. The more knowledge you obtain prior to your purchase will help ensure you buy a tortoise that is right for you and help you avoid making an impulse purchase or poor choice. Sadly, pet shops, expos and breeders may not accurately represent their tortoises. While there are some unscrupulous individuals, most misrepresentations are the result of the vendors own lack of knowledge or because importers did not receive accurate information from collectors. Due to the confusion in classification of the tortoises in the genus *Testudo*, it is even more important to obtain accurate information.

The major issue in purchasing a tortoise is the unknown. If you purchase over the Internet, you rely on the vendor to select your tortoise. While you may get a photo e-mailed to you, it is not the same as being able to examine multiple tortoises before making your selection. If problems arise after your purchase it may be difficult to resolve. Some common sense should be used when buying over the Internet. I would also be wary of sending deposits for future offspring. There are numerous stories of breeders accepting deposits and never being able to produce the promised hatchlings. A reputable breeder will refund the deposit, however many people have lost out on both the tortoise and their deposit.

Some individuals will intentionally misrepresent their animals or even offer illegal specimens. Anyone can claim to be a breeder and represent that they have captive-hatched animals, when in reality their animals are recent imports or brokered from another breeder. Breeders may not know the origin of their founder stock and even if the importer reported the country of origin, this may not be accurate.

Please remember that even a healthy tortoise may become stressed from shipping or become stressed in its new environment. A change in temperature, substrate, and diet may result in a runny nose or lack of appetite for a few days as the tortoise becomes acclimated to its new environment.

A reputable vendor (pet shop, expo, or breeder) will generally provide some limited warranty. This may be 24 hours upon receipt of the animal or much longer. If the vendor is well-known and has been in business for an extended period, they generally will stand behind their sales. If you notice a problem with your tortoise, you should notify the vendor immediately to resolve the issue. They may advise you to wait and see if conditions improve, have you take it to a veterinarian, or ship it back. Often the issue is simply a lack of appetite or activity as it adjusts to its new environment. The prompt notice however is important if the condition becomes worse and a refund is required. You would expect to receive a longer guarantee on a captive-hatched or long-term captive tortoise than on a recent import.

It is recommended that you quarantine any new tortoise for at least three months to monitor its health and reduce the risk that it will contaminate existing collections. Wild-caught imports should be taken to a veterinarian for a fecal examination and treated for parasites. Long-term captive or captive-hatched tortoises that are of good weight and appear healthy may not require a veterinarian visit unless they develop some symptoms of an illness (runny nose, swollen eyes, loose stools, etc.).

Chapter TWO: Outdoor Enclosures

Multiple pens are created in a neighborhood back yard for various species of Mediterranean tortoises. Each separate pen includes grass, hide boxes, water dishes, and elevation changes plus multiple hide areas. All the pens are protected by a fence to ensure dogs or children don't injure a tortoise. Photo by Jerry Fife.

Maintaining your Russian tortoise outdoors is recommended, even if it is only for a portion of the year. One of the positive attributes of Mediterranean tortoises is their ability to handle a wide range of temperatures. In Phoenix, Arizona, I am able to keep Hermann's, Greeks, Marginated, and Russian tortoises outdoors year round as annual temperatures range from a low in winter of approximately 20 to 25° F (-4 to -7°C) to a high in summer of 115-120° F (46-49°C). If local temperatures do not drop much below freezing during the winter months, you may be able to keep your tortoise outdoors all year. The tortoises will hibernate naturally under these conditions, however some keepers prefer to bring tortoises indoors to hibernate them artificially. Artificial hibernation and natural hibernation each have their own pro's and con's and should be based on factors such as temperature extremes, rainfall, and predators in your specific area.

A creative outdoor pen for keeping tortoises near Tulsa, Oklahoma. Courtesy of Linda Putnam. Photo by Russ Gurley.

Each species can handle slightly different temperature ranges. Russian tortoises and species native to the coldest temperature zones can handle more extreme temperatures than the Greek or Marginated tortoises which are native to more temperate zones. If you live in an area where winters are mild and summers are warm, an outdoor set up is very simple for Russian tortoises. The amount of rainfall in your area will impact the design of the enclosure or could prevent year round housing outdoors.

Tortoise enclosures may be created from concrete block, wood, chain link fence, or other building materials. Inside the tortoise enclosure there should be a hide box, areas for basking, grassy areas, and various shrubs.

The outdoor enclosure should be as big as possible, however at least 10 square feet per tortoise should be provided for adult Russian tortoises. If you have large trees or fencing that prevents sun from reaching basking areas, the enclosure will need to be enlarged or the obstructions removed. Tortoises should be protected from dogs or

In some areas, tortoise keepers will have to provide their tortoises with covered, secure pens. These enclosures prevent loss from predators and can also be used to provide some shade. Photo by Jerry Fife.

other animals that may kill or injure them. A chain link fence may provide protection from a dog, however a raccoon might climb the fence quite easily. Raccoons are the top predator of captive turtles and tortoises in the United States. Many keepers are alarmed to hear that backyard tortoises can be killed by birds, cats, dogs, foxes, and even ants. Be aware of potential predators in your area and protect your tortoises.

Also, the enclosure should really be created from a solid material. A visual barrier will keep your tortoise from wanting to walk along a fence and will prevent injury from trying to walk through a fence. My preference is concrete block (8"x 8"x16") because they provide a barrier that the tortoise can't push through or see through plus it does not deteriorate like wood will in the intense Arizona sun. It has been shown that a visual barrier makes a tortoise less likely to want along a fence line. Thinner fence block will work for Russian tortoises, but it is not as sturdy and may be toppled over by a dog, a larger tortoise, or even strong winds. The enclosure should be two blocks high or 16 inches high. The concrete blocks can also be easily moved to expand the pen. If block is used, be sure to cover the corners so the tortoises cannot climb out of the enclosure. There are many elaborate enclosures, however people have had success keeping and even breeding Russian tortoises in some very basic enclosures.

The enclosure should have a variety of shrubs and bushes to provide the tortoise protection from the elements, to provide a feeling of security, and to provide visual barriers for females and subordinate males to escape aggressive males. Plants provide sight barriers and allow tortoises to feel more secure. The pen should be planted with grass or alfalfa for the tortoises to eat, but it should also have some dirt or mounding where the female tortoise will dig to lay her eggs. Some rolling terrain is good as tortoises often bask on slopes to maximize sun exposure or dig into slopes to lay eggs. A water dish should be provided at all times as tortoises will drink standing water but it should be checked daily and cleaned as required. An automatic bubbler system, used to water shrubs, will also work well to provide tortoises with drinking water. Some keepers will just run a garden hose in a low area for a few minutes 3-4 times a week to allow the tortoises to drink.

The need for multiple sight barriers is extremely important for Russian tortoises as they can be aggressive during courtship and mating. Female tortoises need areas where they are able to avoid or escape a persistent male. Often separate enclosures will be required for each sex. This will protect females from aggressive males, except during breeding introductions, and will let a breeder monitor breeding and plan for eggs.

Average low temperatures in Phoenix, Arizona look fairly mild, however there are five months of the year where temperatures may drop below freezing. There are also five months where high temperatures may exceed 115° F (46° C). Generally, even on days where temperatures drop below freezing, temperatures will rise above 50 to 60° F (10 to 15°C) once the sun comes out.

Russians tortoises have been successfully kept outdoors in a line south of Raleigh, South Carolina, Little Rock, Arkansas, Oklahoma City, Oklahoma, Flagstaff, Arizona, and so on . . . without

Weather Details: **Phoenix, Arizona UNITED STATES**
Tropical: Hot and Arid

	J	**F**	**M**	**A**	**M**	**J**	**J**	**A**	**S**	**O**	**N**	**D**
Record High Temp.	88	91	100	106	115	122	120	117	116	107	97	88
Record Low Temp.	16	25	25	35	39	48	63	57	46	34	27	21
Avg. Daily Minimum	41	45	49	55	64	73	81	80	73	61	49	42
Avg. Daily Maximum	66	71	76	85	94	104	106	104	98	88	75	66
Rainfall	.67	.68	.88	.22	.12	.13	.83	.96	.86	.65	.66	1.0

Temperatures are in degrees Farhenheit and Rainfall is in inches.

* Source: www.weather.com

any supplemental heat. These tortoises hibernate naturally and eggs have incubated and hatched naturally from the ground in the tortoise enclosure. Due to the low rainfall, especially here in Arizona, pens are watered and non-native vegetation is provided. Protection must be provided from extreme low and high temperatures. This protection takes the form of a hide box which provides shade on hot days, protection from freezing temperatures during the winter, and shelter from rain.

Hide Box

A hide box provides a secure area where the tortoise can escape from the sun and extreme temperatures as well as the rain. The hide box will also be used during hibernation. Burrowing into foun-

A hide box created from half of a dog travel crate. Photo by Amanda Ebenhack.

tain grass or other shrubs provides the tortoise a sense of security; however it may not provide adequate protection during wet and cold weather. The hide box should be filled with hay or grass clippings to help the tortoise feel more secure. This material also provides insulation for the tortoise during hibernation. The top of the hide box may be made of wood or corrugated metal. The height of the box only needs to be a few inches higher than the dome of the tortoise.

The width and length of the box will be determined by how many tortoises and the size of the tortoises using the box. Generally, a 12" x 12" x 6" tall hide box is sufficient for a pair of Russian tortoises. The opening to the hide box may be covered with strips of plastic (carpet protection runners cut into strips work well) overlapped to allow the tortoise easy entry and to help stabilize the inside temperature, however this is not necessary unless protection from rainfall or extreme cold temperatures are a concern.

The substrate under the box should be sandy soil which drains well, and in which the tortoise can dig to lay eggs. Eggs will fre-

Large enclosures for breeding tortoises in sunny Arizona. Courtesy of Jeff and Kim Gee. Photo by Bob Ashley.

quently be deposited in the soil under the hide box. Sometimes commercial dog houses or "dog igloos" are used by tortoise breeders. These are effective in keeping out the rain, however if the base of the house is left on, it should be filled with at least six inches of soil so the tortoise can burrow in for hibernation or to lay eggs. The hide box must be located where it will not flood from rain. Though some moisture is desirable during spring and summer, conditions should remain relatively dry during cooler months and especially during hibernation.

Chapter THREE: Indoor Enclosures and Hatchling Care

A simple enclosure for a hatchling Russian tortoise. Photo by Russ Gurley.

The preferred setup for adult tortoises is outdoors, however if you live in a location where this is not possible, they can be housed indoors. Due to their small size, many of the Mediterranean tortoises are great candidates for indoor housing. Even if housed indoors the majority of the year, it is still advisable to put the tortoise outdoors for a portion of the summer when weather permits.

The type of indoor housing and space requirement depends on the amount of time the tortoise will be living indoors, the size of the tortoise, and the number of tortoises.

Hatchlings may be raised exclusively inside. This allows better monitoring of food intake, temperature control, and protection from predators. Since most people purchase their tortoise as a small hatchling, the care and maintenance of hatchlings is perhaps most critical. While tortoises can handle a wide range of environments, the first couple of years are important to ensuring long-term health and proper shell development.

Various species of *Testudo* may be kept together as hatchlings, however wild caught specimens or adults must be separated by species. Photo by Jerry Fife.

Care of Hatchlings

A major concern associated with raising captive-hatched tortoises is pyramiding. Pyramiding can be defined as the raising of scutes during active growing periods. During normal growth, each scute (plate of divisions or the shell) increases in size horizontally, thus increasing the overall diameter of each scute and the overall size of the tortoise. In nature, this scute enlargement brings about smooth growth. During dry or cold seasons there will be little or no growth and a slight ridge or ring will develop. This ridge is often referred to as a growth ring and sometimes is used to help determine how old the tortoise is. In a tortoise that is developing pyramiding, this new growth increases the size of the scute in a vertical direction thus raising the scutes. This "pyramiding" is not desirable and is not common in nature for Russian tortoises.

To prevent pyramiding in hatchling tortoises a proper diet and microclimate with a high humidity level is required. To maintain

Creating a Moist Hide to Prevent
Pyramiding in Young Tortoises

Step One: Establish a dry side with grass clippings, 1/2 sand and 1/2 peat moss mixture, etc. and another section with moistened peat moss.

Step Two: Place a plastic shoe box "cave" over the moist area.

The hatchling and young tortoises will spend a good deal of time hiding in the moist moss. This will keep their shell growth smooth and natural as the shell remains pliable during the fast growth stage.

high moisture and humidity levels without creating problems associated with increased levels of bacteria, fungi and mold a microclimate may be developed in the hatchling's habitat. This microhabitat can be made by providing a plastic shoebox with an opening cut in the side, which serves as an entrance. Inside the box should be a one to two inch layer of slightly moist peat moss for the tortoises to hide in. Sphagnum peat moss works well as a moisture-retaining substrate. The peat moss should be soaked in spring water and then squeezed tightly to force out all the extra water. It should be moist but not soaked. As it dries, it will turn lighter in color, alerting the keeper than moisture needs to be added. Peat moss has acidic properties that discourage the growth of molds and fungi. It also doesn't seem to be toxic if ingested and doesn't impact the gut if eaten. Also, it is readily available and relatively inexpensive. The moist peat moss provides the microclimate inside the hide box which is necessary to prevent pyramiding. To maintain the environmental moisture or humidity inside the hide box, the peat moss must be changed regularly or water must be added as needed.

The substrate outside the hide box can be any commonly used dry substrate. Hay such as Bermuda, timothy, or alfalfa hay (with the thick stems removed) will work well. The

A large (3' x 6') *Testudo* enclosure that provides plenty of space for exercise. Photo by Russ Gurley.

dry substrate must be separated from the moisture chamber/hide box to prevent the growth of mold on the dry substrate. It is also important to provide heat, UVB lighting, and a well-balanced diet. The peat moss should be checked routinely for moisture level and regularly replaced with fresh damp peat moss. Under these conditions pyramiding can be eliminated and your young tortoises will remain active and healthy.

Various species of *Testudo* may be kept together as hatchlings, however adults and especially wild-caught specimens should be separated by species.

I suggest that hatchling tortoises be maintained indoors for the first year or two with regular supervised visits to the outdoors. Hatchling tortoises can be maintained in a large glass terrarium, a Waterlandtubs land enclosure, a large blanket box, or a homemade enclosure such as a "Tortoise Table". The enclosure should be lit with a quality UVB-emitting bulb and there should be a heat lamp on one end of the enclosure to provide a basking spot for the tortoise. Be very careful if you do this in a blanket box or a glass terrarium as both can heat up very quickly and cause the death of your tortoise. Often a small (25- or 40-watt bulb) will be enough to provide this warmth, depending on the surrounding circumstances.

The basking spot should be between 85 and 95° F (29 and 35° C). The temperature at night should be above 70° F (21° C) and daytime temperatures above 80° F (27° C). The basking light is necessary so the tortoises can elevate its body temperature to the optimal temperature necessary for digestion. If the tortoises are maintained at a constant ambient temperature, it should be above 80° F (27° C) for Russian tortoises.

Sand or cedar chips should never be used as a substrate for your tortoise. A mixture of 1/2 play sand and 1/2 peat moss is ideal but paper towel, corrugated cardboard, grass clippings, or hay work fine.

A glass terrarium should not be in the direct sun where the temperature inside can increase to unacceptable temperatures. A naturalistic terrarium with plants and rocks may improve the cage's appearance; however the microclimate with a hide box or moisture

An excellent indoor tortoise habitat created inside a Waterlandtub land enclosure. Photo by Amanda Ebenhack.

chamber, proper lighting and temperatures must be maintained. The cage substrate, whether a sand/peat moss mix, potting soil (without ANY additives), dirt, grass clippings, or hay must be changed at least monthly and more frequently if the enclosure is small or multiple tortoises are kept in the enclosure.

Hatchling tortoises should be fed daily. Generally they do best in a routine where they eat in the morning after they have basked under a heat lamp and raised their body temperature to the desired level. Hatchlings may be fed the same diet as the adults but the food items may need to be chopped or shredded small enough so the young tortoise can easily eat it. I don't recommend that water be kept in the enclosure with hatchling tortoises. Every few days the tortoise should be placed in a container with shallow, slightly warm water. The depth of the water should be shallow enough so the tortoise can easily extend its head out of the water. Soak the tortoise 10 to 15 minutes. The tortoise will generally drink and defecate while being soaked. The tortoise should be removed once it defecates so it will avoid drinking the dirty water.

With proper care, your hatchling Russian tortoise should grow approximately 1 to 2 inches per year. The rate of growth can be

A "Tortoise Table" - a handmade enclosure for Mediterranean tortoises. A sturdy screen top will keep pets, children, and unwanted guests out of the enclosure. Photo by Amanda Ebenhack.

accelerated by maintaining warm temperatures and maximizing the amount of food provided. You typically do not need to be concerned with over-feeding hatchlings. In nature these tortoises generally hatch when food is abundant. The hatchling will eat until it is full, and then retire to the hide box to sleep.

Multiple hatchlings may be kept together in the same enclosure without fear of aggression. Be sure to monitor weight and growth of each specimen to ensure all tortoises are getting sufficient food.

Indoor Enclosures for Adults

While outdoor exposure is desirable, Russian tortoises can be housed and maintained indoors either temporarily or permanently. Stock tanks, plastic pools, tubs, and "Tortoise Tables" have been successfully used as indoor enclosures. Some keepers will turn a whole room or basement over to their tortoises. Mediterranean tortoises, due to their relatively small size, are more easily housed indoors and cared for than most tortoise species. The larger the area provided, the longer you will be able to go between cleaning and changing substrates. A clean environment is critical to maintaining a healthy tortoise.

Even for a small tortoise, a large area has advantages. A small enclosure may limit the natural movement of the tortoise or prohibit the ability to provide temperature variations and require more frequent changing of the substrate. A small enclosure does have the advantage of letting the keeper better monitor certain activity, such as food intake and may be helpful when caring for a sick or injured specimen.

If your tortoises are maintained indoors year round, the enclosure must meet all the tortoise's basic requirements. These include lighting (UV and heat), microclimates (humidity and temperature), multiple hiding areas, water, food, and visual barriers if both male and female adult specimens are kept.

It is not recommended that hatchling Russian tortoises be kept with adult specimens due to the significant difference in size. The adult may injure the hatchling or the hatchling may not be able to adequately compete for food.

Chapter FOUR: Hibernation

Tortoises hibernating under the snow in outdoor pens in Illinois. Photo by Mighty J.

In nature, Russian tortoises hibernate. The actual length of hibernation depends on the species, climate, and geographic origin. The most common period of hibernation is October to March. During this time the tortoises bury themselves into the soil and their heart rates slow, reducing their oxygen consumption. This allows them to survive for long periods without food during the winter.

Note: Four to six weeks prior to hibernation the tortoise should be fed high energy food, with plenty of Vitamins A and D3. Vitamin A especially becomes depleted during hibernation; it's stored in the body tissues, fat, and liver and the tortoise draws upon it while asleep. Provide carbohydrate containing foods such as grated carrots, squash, and alfalfa; all which contains Vitamin A.

Prior to hibernation, as the weather becomes cooler, the tortoises will eat less, bask less, and become sluggish. The tortoise will then dig into the soil, or crawl into a burrow or other suitable hiding area which provides it protection from the cold winter weather and rain.

In captivity these same conditions must be provided. If they cannot be provided naturally they must be created artificially.

There is some debate on whether captive tortoises need to hibernate. Some keepers have been successful in maintaining and even breeding species that normally hibernate without subjecting the tortoises to a period of cold hibernation, however most keepers will provide a period of cooling every year for reptile species which become dormant in the wild. This period of dormancy is often critical to reproductive cycles and some species cannot be bred successfully without it.

Many tortoises die during artificial hibernation. This may be due to a number of factors, but is most commonly the result of incorrect temperatures (too hot or too cold) or the condition of the tortoise prior to hibernation. Due to the risk associated with hibernation, a sick or injured tortoise or one with poor weight should not be hibernated. Hibernation is also more risky for hatchlings or small tortoises due to their lack of body mass which makes them more susceptible to temperature fluctuations. For this reason, I believe that hatchling tortoises should not be put into hibernation their first year or they should be hibernated for a shorter period. Skipping hibernation occasionally, even for adults, does not appear to create any long-term problems for a tortoise and is much less risky than attempting to hibernate a weak or sick animal.

Artificial Hibernation

For artificial hibernation, a variety of methods and containers are used effectively. The tortoise may be hibernated in an unheated shed, a basement, or in an old refrigerator. The tortoise may be placed in a plastic shoe box, styrofoam cooler, or similar container with several ventilation holes added. The size of the container depends on the size of the tortoise. It may also be advantageous to place this box in a larger container to provide added protection. Place several inches of top soil mixed with fresh sphagnum peat moss (Fresh peat moss maintains a slight moisture which provides some humidity) in the bottom of the container and cover this with several inches of leaves, grass clippings, hay, or sphagnum moss. The hibernating tortoise is going to try to reach a "microclimate" when it digs into the soil. An

80% soil humidity seems to be the norm. Don't confuse soil humidity with wet soil. Lengthy periods of cold, wet conditions will kill your tortoise.

The container should be placed in a dark cool area away from any heat source and protected from any predators. Some keepers prefer to use a towel or shredded newspaper for a substate as hay or other organic material may mold. The substrate helps the tortoise maintain its core temperature, even if there are slight temperature fluctuations. It also helps the tortoise dig in and feel secure. The tortoise does not need to bury under the substrate. If it is not totally covered it permits easier observation during hibernation.

The temperature of the room (hibernaculum) housing the hibernating tortoise should be maintained between 39 and 50° F (4 and 10° C). Tortoises exposed to temperatures below this may experience post-hibernation anorexia, limb damage, eye problems, or even death. A thermometer which measures maximum and minimum temperatures is a useful investment. If the tortoise is kept too warm - above 50° F (10° C) - and becomes active, it will consume its fat reserves during hibernation resulting in weight loss, dehydration, and a buildup of toxins and uric acid. I think the ideal temperature for indoor incubation for a Russian tortoise is 41° F (5° C) as the tortoise will use little energy, therefore producing little waste.

Note: These temperature ranges are for ideal indoor incubation. In an outdoor situation, temperatures will get cooler but if the tortoise has buried itself properly under a shelter, it will be fine.

Weigh your tortoise, then record and monitor the weight during hibernation. An adult tortoise should lose about 1% of its pre-hibernation weight each month while hibernating. A significant weight loss indicates something is wrong and the tortoise should be brought out of hibernation. If the tortoise urinates while hibernating the loss of fluids indicates a problem which should cause the tortoise to be taken out of hibernation. The tortoise may pass fecal material during hibernation. The tortoise can be checked weekly and weighed weekly to monitor its status.

These leaf-filled tubs in a cool basement provide the ideal indoor hibernation area for a group of Hermann's tortoises. Photo by Torsten Blanck.

Caution should be used when selecting the location for hibernation. A refrigerator in a garage or other unprotected area may still drop to unsafe temperatures. Remember that refrigerators do not have heating elements, and it must be able to maintain a constant temperature in the desired range. Use of outdoors sheds, etc. must also be protected from rats or other animals that could harm the hibernating tortoise. If a refrigerator is used, it must be opened periodically to ensure adequate ventilation or air flow.

The length of hibernation required for captive tortoises is subject to debate. A Russian tortoise in Kazakhstan may stay underground for all but three months of the year. In other areas, this species may hibernate for only 3 months. The length of hibernation in nature is obviously dependent on the climate and annual variations. In captivity, under artificial conditions, a hibernation of two to four months is sufficient for all Russian tortoises. The length of hibernation may be influenced by the size of the tortoise, species or origin of the tortoise, or the experience and comfort level of the hobbyist.

Due to the risk of hibernation, some keepers want to minimize the time period for hibernation, while other keepers enjoy the break or want to extend hibernation until warm weather permits moving the tortoises outdoors. I think a two month long hibernation is adequate. In cool climates this may mean that tortoises will need to be kept indoors before and/or after hibernation until outdoor temperatures allow return to their outside enclosures.

Preparing a healthy tortoise for hibernation will involve several steps to mimic what occurs in nature.

1. Reduce food supply for four weeks prior to hibernation.

A reduction in the quantity of food provided during this period will help prevent undigested food from decomposing in the stomach over the hibernation period. Temperatures must remain warm enough to ensure that the tortoise is able to digest and process its food prior to hibernation. Any undigested food will decay, produce large quantities of gas, and cause tympanic colic, which causes asphyxiation due to internal pressure on the lungs. This is also responsible for serious and usually fatal bacterial infections.

2. At my facility, in September or October (when temperature naturally decrease in the tortoise's native range), is when the hibernation preparations and food reduction takes place. One week following the tortoise's last meal, daytime temperatures should be dropped about 10 degrees a week for three weeks. Reduce/cool temperatures from 80° to 70° F, 70° to 60° F, 60° to 50° F, and so on. Nighttime temperatures may be 5 to 10 degrees Fahrenheit lower than the daytime temperatures. During this time, the tortoise may be soaked to ensure it eliminates all feces and urine. This will also ensure proper hydration prior to entering hibernation. The tortoise should be dried following soakings to make sure it is not damp when entering hibernation.

3. Allow access to water or soak the tortoise to aid evacuation of the gut two or three times in the week before hibernation. (Dry the tortoise thoroughly following soakings during cool down period.)

4. Record the weight of the tortoise as it goes into hibernation and each week during hibernation.

5. Hibernate the tortoise in a container with peat moss, grass clippings, hay, etc. at a temperature between 40 - 50° F (4 - 10° C) for 2 to 4 months. As discussed earlier, this can be achieved by placing the container in a cool garage, basement, or in a modified refrigerator, depending on where you live. Many reptile keepers cool their reptiles in a wine cooler. This also works well as these chillers have a thermostat to control the temperature.

* Many wine coolers have a maximum temperature setting of 55° F, ideal for hibernating many Mediterranean tortoises as long as they are being monitored closely. Be sure to open the cooler once a week or more to allow some air exchange.

6. After the hibernation period, remove the container from hibernation temperatures. Allow the container to warm slowly for a few hours.

7. Place the tortoise into a heated indoor enclosure with recommended temperatures of 80° F (27° C) with a hot spot of 95° F (35° C).

Golden Greek tortoises will bury in the dirt to hibernate and can handle the Arizona winters with occasional temperatures down below 20° F. Photo by Jerry Fife.

8. Offer water or soak the tortoise in slightly warm water daily for a week after hibernation.

9. If your tortoise does not resume normal feeding behavior, has lost significant weight, or has discharge from its nose or eyes take your tortoise to a veterinarian.

Tortoises are cold-blooded and in cold weather they cannot warm up enough to digest food. They regulate their body temperature by basking in the sun to warm up or hiding in burrows or under cover to cool if temperatures are too hot. If temperatures are optimal, the tortoise is active and will feed and is able to digest its food.

Once warmed up and provided with a basking spot (85 to 95° F) to thermoregulate, the tortoise may be offered food. The tortoise will generally eat after a couple of days. If the tortoise does not eat within one week, or if it remains sluggish, has lost significant weight, or has discharge, it may need to be checked by a veterinarian.

Outdoor Hibernation

In Phoenix and much of the southern United States, tortoises may be hibernated outdoors. I have successfully hibernated Russian tor-

A large female Russian tortoise emerging from hibernation. Photo by Gary Bright.

toises outdoors for many years. In Phoenix, Arizona the average rainfall during the months of hibernation is less than an inch each month. The low temperatures have reached 20° F (-7° C) with typical daytime highs in the 60's or 70's F. Though these temperatures don't seem to fit the artificial hibernation temperatures recommended, these tortoises have naturally hibernated outside for years.

Shelters for tortoises can be provided by using half of a dog crate, wood doghouse, and a variety of other materials. Photo by Russ Gurley.

The hibernation period in Phoenix typically begins in October or November and lasts into February or March. If you live in an area with similar temperatures, natural hibernation may be considered.

To facilitate hibernation for Russian tortoises outdoors, it is important to provide a hide box which is stuffed with hay. The tortoises will dig into the hay and often the ground below the hay. The hide box will provide protection from rain. The hay and soil provide insulation from the freezing temperatures. It is important that the tortoise has access to well-draining soil and an area that does not flood. If provided a large outdoor area with multiple hide boxes and shrubs, the tortoise will be able to find the microclimate that it prefers.

After the hibernation period, once daily minimum temperatures reach about 55° F (13° C), the tortoises will begin to emerge from hibernation. Food is offered and water is provided and tortoises will emerge each morning to bask and raise their body temperature. They will position themselves on a rock or against a wall of the enclosure, and turn their shell to maximize the exposure to the sun. Once they reach their optimal temperature they will eat and then retreat to their hide box. Breeding will begin in the days following hibernation and egg laying will soon follow.

Though tortoises may hibernate in locations which receive snow, if you have significant snow or rain during the winter, artificial hibernation in a more controlled area (indoors) is recommended. Another issue is predators. If there are raccoons, skunks, or other predators active in your area, the enclosure must be protected.

Hobbyists do report success in breeding *Testudo* species without hibernation, and if in doubt you may decide to keep the tortoises warm year-round. The tortoises, however, may still slow down and become less active, eating less, and demonstrating signs that they are trying to hibernate. If this occurs, it should either be allowed to hibernate (if health permits) or temperatures should be checked, and if needed, increased to stimulate more activity. The key factor is if a tortoise is losing weight, a few weeks of inactivity may not be an issue, however if the tortoise is losing weight, temperatures must be adjusted to stimulate activity (eating) or cooled to decrease activity. To stimulate activity, soak the tortoise in warm water and follow the suggestions of bringing a tortoise out of hibernation. If the tortoise does not respond to your manipulation, it should be taken to a veterinarian.

Chapter FIVE: Feeding

A group of Russian tortoises finishing off a head of romaine lettuce. Photo by Jerry Fife.

Russian tortoises will feed on a variety of grasses and vegetation. They require a high fiber diet rich in calcium.

At least 132 species of plants have been identified as food sources for Mediterranean tortoises in the wild (Cheylan, 2001). A clear preference has been shown for species of the daisy family (Asteraceae), bean and acacia family (Fabaceae), plantain family (Plantaginaceae), and to a lesser extent sweet grasses (Poaceae), the crowfoot and buttercup family (Ranunculaceae), and grasses (Graminaceae). It is reported that they also consume some rather dangerously poisonous plants without suffering negative effects. These include Black bryony (*Tamus communis*) and most species of Arum lily (*Arum* species), and mushrooms.

In addition to their main diet of plant matter, Russian tortoises may consume invertebrates such as slugs, snails, earthworms, and caterpillars. They also will feed on carrion and the feces of other

animals including dogs, rabbits, sheep, cattle, and humans. Stomach contents have also included egg shells, bones, feathers, and small pebbles. Tortoises identify food with both the sense of sight and smell. They seem to be attracted to red, orange, and yellow flowers and fruits.

While Mediterranean tortoises should be provided with access to water, their water requirement may be totally covered through the consumption of fresh, juicy plants.

A Russian tortoise enjoying a piece of zucchini squash.

From the above referenced diet for the Russian tortoise, it is apparent that in nature tortoises have access to a much greater variety of plant matter than can be provided in captivity. Though we may not provide over 100 different species of plants, we should try to provide a varied diet, even if we use a few main core food items.

I feed Russian tortoises the following:

Grass – (Bermuda, Rye, Alfalfa, Blue grass, Fescue, etc.)
Opuntia cactus (Spineless prickly pear cactus) High fiber, good calcium to phosphorus ratio

Russian tortoises enjoying a salad of mixed greens and shredded vegetables. Photo by Chris Roscher.

Carrots, Bell peppers, Tomatoes
Various Greens
(Mustard Greens, Escarole, Romaine lettuce, Kale, Dandelion, Bok Choy, etc.)
Squash (Zucchini, Pumpkin, etc.)
Strawberries
Mazuri Tortoise Diet®

Natural grass should be available and supplemented with *Opuntia* cactus, zucchini, and carrots. A closely mowed lawn is preferred for grazing, however taller grass also provides the tortoise shelter from the sun. Some Mediterranean tortoises will not actively graze on grass, preferring broad leaf plants and weeds. A tortoise maintained in an area with adequate natural grass and broadleaf weeds such as dandelions will require minimal supplemental food, however cactus, carrots, squash, and store greens may be provided once or twice a week.

A variety of food items should be available to ensure all dietary needs are met. If maintained outdoors, few if any vitamin supple-

The ideal Russian tortoise salad of mixed greens, some sliced fruit, and shredded vegetables. Photo by Amanda Ebenhack.

ments are required. Calcium may be added to the diet of hatchlings or adult females that may be forming eggs. Cuttlebone may be used as a source of calcium. Some keepers also use oyster shell, egg shell, or animal bones for their tortoises to chew on to help trim their beaks and as a source of calcium. While adding calcium powder to the diet of hatchlings or females developing eggs may be beneficial, it is not needed for adult males.

Hatchlings may be fed the same food items as adults. I feed hatchlings and young tortoises food that is shredded or chopped for easy consumption. Calcium powder should be sprinkled over the chopped salad once a week. Mazuri Tortoise Diet® is also a good source of food for hatchlings and adults. The Tortoise Diet® should be soaked for a few minutes and then the excess water drained. The Tortoise Diet® will have a spongy consistency and is easily con-sumed by hatchlings and small tortoises. Tortoise Diet® may also be included in the diet of adult tortoises.

Hatchlings will develop a routine feeding response if fed at the same time each day. Generally, a hatchling tortoise will bask to raise its body temperature, eat, and then return to its shelter to sleep during the heat of the day.

Foods to Avoid

Avoid feeding any plants or vegetables high in oxalates, especially to hatchlings and adult females producing eggs. Beet greens, spinach, rhubarb and chard contain oxalates. Oxalic acid binds with calcium to yield insoluble calcium oxalate which cannot be absorbed by the tortoise. Cabbage, collards, kale, and broccoli can cause goiters if fed in excess as they tie up iodine.

Fruit should be fed sparingly to tortoises as it raises lactic acid levels in the gut and promotes intestinal parasites, colic, and loose droppings.

Canned or dry dog and cat food should not be fed to tortoises. The digestion of a high protein diet may cause kidney problems, reducing the lifespan of the tortoise.

If the tortoise is healthy, has a varied diet or mainly feeds on natural grass, the occasional consumption of these food items is acceptable. If the tortoise has existing health problems such as a soft shell, parasites, runny stool, or other health issues, these questionable foods could further impact the condition. A tortoise on the correct diet should have well-formed fibrous droppings. A diet solely of store greens with high water content may also result in runny stools.

Protein

There are a number of opinions on the cause of pyramiding. Many have assumed that excessive protein in the diet was the cause of pyramiding. Since this was the common assumption, it followed that protein should be all but eliminated from the diet. This, however, is not the case. Though carrion or some animal matter may be eaten in nature, this is not required in captivity if a varied diet is offered. Don't be surprised to see your tortoise chew on a dead animal, if available.

Water

Water may be provided by various methods. A keeper can use a water dish, drip system, hose, or bubbler system. A garden hose may be allowed to run in a depression in the pen where tortoises will drink. This should be done once or twice a week, depending on the time of the year (twice a week in the hottest part of the summer and once a week in the cooler months). Others prefer to provide a water dish due to soil or temperature conditions. Be sure to check your water dish daily to ensure it has not been overturned or become a breeding ground for bacteria and mosquitoes. It should also be checked to ensure the tortoises have not defecated in the water. The dish should be cleaned with a light bleach solution and left in the sun to dry.

Hatchlings should be soaked in shallow, slightly warm water a couple times a week. The young tortoises will drink and often defecate during their soaking. Even if they don't drink, it does encourage defecation and passing of uric acid. Once they defecate they should be removed to prevent them from drinking the dirty water. Adult tortoises should also be provided with the opportunity to soak periodically.

Other Foods

Often new tortoise owners will call and say, "My tortoise will only eat watermelon. It refuses to eat anything else". Tortoises will develop preferences for certain food items and may develop poor eating habits and refuse to eat the correct food items. If only fed their favorite foods, such as watermelon, strawberries, banana, lettuce, etc. they may refuse to eat other items which are needed for proper nourishment. These favorite food items should be removed and other items offered. Generally, the tortoise will begin eating a wider range of food, however if they refuse, their diet may be slowly changed by offering a food salad. Finely chopped food items may be added to their favorite food items and the percentage slowly increased until they accept an improved diet. Remember that grass should be a portion of a Russian tortoise's diet. If they will not graze you should stop offering other food items or begin the process to introduce grass or other high fiber items into their diet.

Following are some food items which have beneficial properties for tortoises and other herbivores:

Alfalfa (*Medicago sativa*) - Retards the development of streptozoto-cin diabetes in some animals, encourages blood clotting, and reduces uric acid. Aids in weight gain and works as a binding agent for diarrhea. It is high in chlorophyll and nutrients. It alkalizes and detoxifies the body, and is good for anemia, hemorrhaging, arthritis, pituitary gland function, and contains antifungal agents. Keepers have often avoided alfalfa due to its protein content, however it is a good food source, both live and dried.

Aloe vera - Though this is listed by some as being a toxic plant, some tortoises do eat it. It has immunity enhancing properties and is also a laxative, antiseptic, and antifungal. It works on the thyroid, the pituitary gland, and the ovaries.

Artichoke (*Cynara scolymus*) - Leaves help detoxify the liver and aids digestion. Contains silymarin, the same as Milk thistle, which acts as a natural antibiotic.

Carrot (*Daucus carota*) - A natural diuretic and stimulant, anti-inflammatory, and antiseptic. Carrots cleanse the system of impurities and are useful in the treatment of respiratory conditions. They may also help to overcome many glandular disorders. They are high in beta-carotene, the precursor to Vitamin A. The juice of a carrot contains sugar, starch, extractine gluten, albumen, volatile oil, pectin, saline matter, malic acid, and carotene. They are rich in Vitamins A, B, C, and E and the minerals phosphorus, potassium, and calcium. Carrots have been used as a natural dewormer and laxative.

Celery (*Apium graveolens*) - Celery is a mild diuretic and clears uric acid from painful joints. It is a tonic for liver problems, stimulates the thyroid and pituitary glands, and is possibly an antioxidant. It also has anti-inflammatory properties.

Cucumber (*Cucumis sativus*) - The leaves and fruit aid intestinal ailments. Dietary value is questionable as they are made up of around 96% water. The seeds are said to act as a natural dewormer, a mild diuretic, and kidney tonic. It is also used as an anti-inflammatory. Due to questionable food value, cucumbers should be fed only sparingly. Cucumbers may be helpful to encourage a tortoise to eat which has refused to eat.

Dandelion (*Taraxacum officinale*) - Of all the so-called "weeds", this is a popular plant in tortoise feeding as it contains high amounts of Vitamin A. It aids digestive regularity and has beneficial effects in hepatic disorders, chronic inflammation, and enlargement of the liver. It increases the bile flow in animals and has a stimulating effect on liver and gall bladder secretion. Dandelions act as a powerful diuretic to treat urinary disorders and fluid retention without depleting potassium and stimulate the excretion of toxins.

Fig (*Ficus carica*) - Figs can be used as a mild laxative and as a demulcent. The stalk of the ripe fruit is said to have antibiotic properties. They are highly alkaline, and contain a powerful healing agent, are antifungal, anti-inflammatory, and contain a bactericide. Figs help to soothe respiratory ailments, ease digestive complaints, and are said to help prevent cancer. As with all fruit, figs should be fed sparingly.

Grape (*Vitis vinifera*) - The leaves are astringent and are sometimes used to stop bleeding and as a cure for dysentery in cattle. The leaves contain cane sugar and glucose, tartaric acid, potassium bi-tartrate, quercetine, quercitrin, tannin, amidon, malic acid, inosite, an uncrystallizable fermentable sugar, and oxalate of calcium. Ripe fruit acts as a diuretic if fed in excess. Ripe grapes in quantity influence the kidneys, producing a free flow of urine, and are a stimulant. The ripe fruit contains sugar, gum, malic acid, potassium bi-tartrate, and inorganic salts. Raisins contain dextrose and potassium acid tartrate.

(The author has grape vines growing in his tortoise pens and grape leaves are readily eaten, however access to the fruit should be minimized.)

Lettuce - Lettuce is high in nitrates and is converted in the mouth into compounds that produce nitric oxide, a potent antibacterial chemical. The "disinfectant" effect of this chemical was tested and salivary production was high enough to kill even *E. coli* 0157 (the deadly bacterium that is so often responsible for outbreaks of food poisoning). People often condemn lettuce as a "bad" food, however along with a good balanced diet it can actually be beneficial. What is

NOT recommended is a diet of lettuce alone as this will not provide all the nutrients your tortoise needs.

Papaya (*Carica papaya*) - Papaya acts as a natural laxative. Latex from unripe fruit and also the leaves contains chymopapain, a protein digester used for treating intestinal disorders, and is currently being used in humans on an experimental basis to treat slipped discs.

Pumpkin (*Cucurbita pepo*) - The seeds expel intestinal worms, including tapeworms. Effective agent: Cucurbitin - an amino acid. Also contains L-tryptophan, effective against depression and sleep disorders as well as anxiety in humans.

Red clover (*Trifolium pratense*) - This perennial is often used in pasture mixes and is said to relieve lung congestion and to act as an antispasmodic. Also used against diarrhea. Ingredient: Uzarin, and isoflavone biochanin A which is said to be a potent anti-carcinogenic.

Sweet peppers (*Capsicum annuum*) - Pungent capsaicin serves as a digestive stimulant and stimulates circulation.

Tomato (*Lycopersion esulentum*) - The leaves and stems of the plant are toxic. The fruits contain Vitamin C and can be used as occasional treats as they are said to be a digestive aid.

Violet (*Viola odorata*) - Leaves are used as a respiratory and immune system stimulant and also to cleanse the digestive system. The underground stems and roots are a strong emetic and purgative as they have a higher concentration of a glucoside, Viola-quercitin.

Watercress (*Nasturtium officinale*) - Watercress acts as an expectorant and an appetite stimulant. Encourages immune system activity in the body and is an anti-inflammatory, diuretic, expectorant, and antiseptic. Useful as a preventive measure for chronic respiratory conditions. Provides good supplies of the Vitamins A, C, and B (thiamin and riboflavin), iron, potassium, and calcium.

REFERENCES:

Bremnes, Lesley. 1988. *The Complete Book of Herbs*. Viking Studio Books. New York, USA.

Hey, Barbara. 1998. *The Illustrated Book of Herbs*. Rodale Press.

Pujol, Jean. 1999. *The Herbalist Handbook* - African flora Medicinal Plants.

Reader's Digest. 1986. *Magic and Medicine of Plants: A practical guide to the science, history, folklore and everyday uses of medicinal plants*. Random House: Pleasantville, NY, USA.

van Wyk, Ben-Eric, B. van Oudtshoorn, and N. Gericke. 1997. *Medicinal Plants of South Africa*. Briza Publications. Pretoria. South Africa.

Weiner, Michael A. and Janet A. Weiner. 1994. *Herbs That Heal*. Mill Valley: Quantum Books.

The Merck Veterinary manual – 9th Edition. 2006. Merck & Co., Inc. Whitehouse Station, NJ USA.

Chapter SIX: Health

An inactive Russian tortoise with swollen eyes needs warmth, a good soak, and immediate attention.

Proper husbandry will allow you to avoid or prevent most health issues, however even careful keepers will experience an occasional health problem with their tortoises. If you regularly check your tortoise, you will be able to catch most health issues and correct them before they become a significant issue or result in the death of your tortoise.

Be aware that some diseases, particularly viral diseases, may be difficult to detect until it's too late. Also, a tortoise may be a carrier without displaying any outward symptoms. To prevent exposing your collection to an "asymptomatic carrier" it is recommended that new acquisitions be quarantined away from other tortoises for at least 90 days. Do not mix species and have wild-caught tortoises checked by a qualified veterinarian. A regular fecal examination is also recommended for wild-caught tortoises.

Preventing stress is an important factor in maintaining a healthy immune system for your tortoise. A change in your tortoise's environment, diet, adverse temperatures, and lack of water create stress which will make your tortoise more susceptible to disease and parasites.

Check your tortoise regularly for respiratory distress, weight loss, runny stools, and physical changes. These are all signs of a possible problem. If a tortoise is alert and feeding it is fairly easy for a keeper to treat minor problems. If a tortoise is lethargic and refusing to eat or is suffering from a more serious problem or injury, call your veterinarian.

The **Association of Reptile and Amphibian Veterinarians (ARAV)** is an organization of veterinarians that specialize in reptile and amphibian care. You can access their website at **http://www.arav.com** to find a veterinarian in your area.

Respiratory Ailments

Respiratory problems are the most common ailment seen in captive Russian tortoises.

Respiratory problems occur when a tortoise gets chilled or is kept in sub-optimal conditions. Minor problems can be corrected with heat and a drop in humidity. If not corrected, minor problems can progress to more serious conditions such as pneumonia. Signs of a respiratory problem include labored breathing, a nasal discharge, a gaping mouth, puffy eyes, lethargy, and a loss of appetite.

To correct minor respiratory problems, increase the warmth of the enclosure with an extra heat source such as a fixture with an incandescent bulb or place a heating pad under the enclosure. The added heat will help boost your tortoise's immune system and allow it to better fight infection.

Keep the enclosure hot and dry. Bump up the temperature to 90° F (32° C) and increase the hot spot to 100° F (38° C). During this time, you must make sure to keep the tortoise well-hydrated by soaking the tortoise and ensuring water is available to drink.

Plants and shelters in enclosures provide a sense of security to captive tortoises. This will, in turn, help keep stress-related illnesses to a minimum. Photo by Jerry Fife.

More severe cases or tortoises that do not respond to added heat will typically require a course of antibiotics. Generally, Baytril® (Enrofloxacin) and Garamycin® (Gentomycin) are effective for treating respiratory ailments in turtles and tortoises. Antibiotic drugs must be prescribed by your veterinarian.

Bladder Stones/Urite Wastes

Bladder stones are a potential problem for tortoises that are not well-hydrated or eat a poor diet. To conserve water, tortoises produce insoluble urinary wastes such as uric acid and urate salts. These urate wastes are regularly passed when the tortoise urinates or defecates. Many novice tortoise keepers have questioned when their tortoise passes a whitish chalk- or paste-like substance. This is the tortoise's normal method to pass urates and a sign of good hydration. If the tortoise is dehydrated, the bladder will reabsorb urinary water. The urate wastes will gradually form a solid stone-like substance which may become an impaction to defecation. If the tortoise is unable to pass the bladder stone it may result in paralysis of the hind legs and eventually death. Soaking the tortoise once or twice a week in shallow water will help prevent dehydration and help the tortoise pass urate wastes.

Injuries

Injuries occur in active tortoises, especially aggressive breeders such as Russian tortoises which ram and bite each other frequently, however injuries may also occur from being burned, from being dropped, or from being attacked by dogs or other predators, and very commonly, being hit by a lawnmower. If cuts are not cleaned and protected, maggots may infest the wound, compounding the damage.

A wash of Betadine® works well to promote the healing of minor shell scrapes and injuries and kills off harmful bacteria. Do not use Betadine® on an open wound, as the iodine solution kills much of the healthy skin that should grow and pull the wound back together. Most rehabbers who take care of injured turtles and tortoises now use sterile water instead of Betadine® to clean a wound and use an antibiotic lotion, or Silvadene® ointment, to prevent bacteria growth in and around the wound.

Serious injuries will usually involve a visit to your veterinarian as they might require stitches, gauze wraps, or even fixators for severe shell damage (Ebenhack, 2011). Fiberglass is no longer used to patch or repair turtle and tortoise shells as it has been shown to trap bacteria and often causes severe infections under the fiberglass (Ebenhack, 2011).

With proper care, tortoises are surprisingly able to recover from significant shell injuries.

Due to courtship and aggressive courtship and mating in Russian tortoises, males and females may need to be separated for part of the year. An aggressive male may kill a young male or a female that is unable to escape. Separation will also allow a female to recover from aggressive ramming and biting inflicted during breeding.

Parasites

Most, if not all, wild-caught tortoises are imported with external and/or internal parasites.

Ticks

If you find a tick on your tortoise, it should be removed. Ticks drain your tortoise of blood and energy, transmit diseases, and can multiply by the hundreds. To remove a tick, grasp it firmly as close to the point of attachment to the tortoise as possible and pull it out. Avoid leaving the head of the tick imbedded in the tortoise's skin. Place a dab of antibiotic lotion on the area where the tick was removed for a few days afterwards.

Internal Parasites

Imported tortoises or those mixed with imported specimens are often plagued by a variety of internal parasites. You can verify an infestation if you see worms or proglottids (worm segments) in a tortoise's feces or by having a fecal check done by your veterinarian. Adult parasitic worms pass many eggs out with a tortoise's feces. In an enclosure, these eggs can infect any tortoise (or other animal) that happens to ingest them on blades of grass, in the soil, in water, etc. These eggs can be seen under a microscope. If your tortoise eats but fails to gain weight or has runny stools, a fecal check is recommended.

Note: Medications should be used only after consulting your veterinarian.

Panacur® (Fenbendazole) and Flagyl® (Metronidazole) may be used to eliminate most parasitic infections. Panacur® works well for roundworms (nematodes) and Flagyl® works well for eliminating amoebic organisms.

Panacure®

Panacur® is recommended for the elimination of parasitic worms.

Panacur® is available as a paste which may be spread on the tortoise's food.

Dosage of Panacur®
25-50 mg / kg
2 ml / kg (2.5%)

* From *Health Care & Rehabilitation of Turtles and Tortoises* by Amanda Ebenhack, (2011) LIVING ART publishing, Ada, OK.

The easiest method to give your tortoise Panacur® is to put it on its favorite food. A piece of fruit or their salad can be covered with the proper dosage of Panacur® and will be consumed by the tortoise. If there are multiple tortoises, care must be taken to ensure each tortoise receives the proper dosage. Tortoises may need to be separated and fed individually to ensure each receives treatment.

Flagyl®

Flagyl® is recommended for the treatment of amoebic parasites and gram-negative bacterial organisms. Flagyl® is available as a liquid or in tablet form.

Dosage of Flagyl® (Metronidazole)
25-50 mg / kg
3 ml / kg (2.3%)

* From *Health Care & Rehabilitation of Turtles and Tortoises* by Amanda Ebenhack, (2011) LIVING ART publishing, Ada, OK.

Caution: Ivermectin®, which is commonly available for treatment of parasites in horses and cattle, will kill tortoises and should not be used. Check with your veterinarian for other treatment options.

Weight loss or runny stools may be an indication of a potential problem. A fecal sample may be taken to your veterinarian to determine what treatment is required. Good husbandry and hygiene will help you avoid infections.

Soft Shell

Soft shell is a severe problem in hatchling tortoises that results from the lack of direct sunlight and calcium. The tortoise's blood stream robs calcium from its bones and shell to meet the calcium needs of the muscles and other body systems, leaving the tortoise's shell soft and pliable. This condition can be corrected by adding calcium and vitamin supplements to its food and ensuring UVB requirements are met. This problem generally occurs in tortoises kept indoors which are not exposed to natural sunlight. Even if the tortoise is given a calcium supplement, it must have exposure to natural sunlight or UVB light to be able to process and use the available calcium.

The reduced shell collagen and the "mushy shell" condition also commonly occurs when juvenile tortoises are fed a protein deficient diet (especially one consisting solely of lettuce and fruit).

Viruses

Russian tortoises have been known to be hosts of viruses representing the genera *Herpesvirus, Iridovirus, Paramyxovirus,* and *Sendaivirus*. It appears that they are particularly susceptible to infections with *Herpesviru*s. Both captive and wild tortoises have tested positive for mycoplasma. Some tortoises may test positive for mycoplasma without showing any external signs.

Tortoises which test positive should be isolated from any other tortoises. Mycoplasmosis affects primarily the upper respiratory tract, resulting in Upper Respiratory Tract Disease (URTD) which can be spread by direct contact between tortoises. The disease is difficult to treat and long-term prognosis is not good. Some tortoises do seem to be able to clear the organism, but may harbor the bacteria within the nasal cavities for years, suffering regular recurrences, particularly when stressed.

Abnormal Growth of a Tortoise's Beak or Nails

Abnormal growth of a tortoise's beak or nails is uncommon in wild tortoises, however it is sometimes encountered in captive specimens. An overgrown beak or nails usually indicates an underlying nutritional deficiency. However, some tortoises develop long toe nails as normal secondary sex characteristics. An overgrown beak can be caused by nutritional secondary hyperparathyroid disease - a form of metabolic bone disease (MBD) - resulting from a gross imbalance in the ratio of calcium and phosphorus in their diet.

In these cases, the parathyroid glands are stimulated to secrete parathormone, which induces the leaching of calcium from the hydroxyapatite crystals in the mature bone matrix, causing malocclusion (the upper and lower beaks do not align). This, again, may be due to diet and MBD which results in distortions of the skull, inappropriate food items (usually a diet of all soft foods), and trauma.

The beak may be trimmed to a normal configuration with a coping tool, Dremel (small motorized sanding tool), file, or emery board. It will also be necessary to correct the underlying cause of the abnormal growth, such as lack of calcium, feeding too many soft foods, etc. If the problem cannot be corrected due to advancement of MBD, abnormal growth may be an ongoing problem. The beak only needs to be trimmed if it inhibits the tortoise's ability to eat.

Generally, tortoises wear down their beaks and keep them trimmed by chewing on old bones, eating tough plant matter, and a variety of other items. If the basic diet is correct, an overgrown beak likely stems from too much soft food. The problem may be corrected by feeding "chewable food", providing cuttlebone to chew, or adding bones to the enclosure which the tortoise may chew. The cuttlebone serves two purposes. Not only does it help wear down the beak but it is also a good source of calcium. While some tortoises will ignore the bones or cuttlebone, others will use it.

If your tortoise does have an overgrown beak, please have it evaluated by your veterinarian. The beak does have a blood and nerve supply, and if trimmed incorrectly, it can cause severe pain, bleeding, and lead to infection which may result in disfigurement or death. Some veterinarians will put the animal on systemic antibiotics prior to trimming the beak. Trimming the beak can be a difficult job as you must secure the tortoise's head so you can carefully file the beak. Depending on the severity of the growth a Dremel may be easier or quicker than a handheld file, however care must be taken to avoid generating too much heat when grinding. It may take two people to successfully complete this task.

A tortoise's nails may also grow excessively long if kept indoors on soft terrain. The tip of the nail may be clipped with a pair of strong nail clippers taking care to not cut the quick of the nail (vein that runs down the nail). If this happens use styptic powder (or baking powder) to stop the bleeding. Adding rough surfaces to the tortoise enclosure (such a rocks and slate) and dirt for digging will allow the tortoise to naturally wear down its nails. Tortoises fed an appropriate diet and kept in outdoor pens generally do not experience abnormal growth of their beaks or nails.

Pyramiding

Pyramiding is a condition of abnormal growth which results in a bumpy carapace or the appearance of "pyramids" on the top of the shell. While natural pyramiding is reported in some species such as Star tortoises, it is not natural in Russian tortoises. Pyramiding is most significant with captive-hatched and raised tortoises. Pyramiding doesn't pose a problem for the tortoise unless dietary deficiencies have contributed to the pyramiding. Extreme pyramiding, in an otherwise healthy tortoise, can hinder the ability of the male tortoise to mount the female thus preventing reproduction. Scutes that have already exhibited pyramiding cannot be corrected, however if conditions for shell development are corrected the new growth can develop normally. The most critical time for pyramiding to develop is during the first year or two of a tortoise's life. If conditions are corrected during this period, the chance of pyramiding developing is greatly reduced even if later husbandry conditions are not optimum.

The chapter on raising hatchlings discusses how to prevent pyramiding and how to ensure smooth natural growth in hatchlings. The key is providing a moisture chamber to ensure adequate levels of humidity are maintained.

The role of humidity in preventing pyramiding, established by chelonian expert Richard Fife through numerous trials in raising hundreds of hatchling African Spurred and Leopard tortoises, has since been confirmed and effectively applied to Russian tortoises and other species. This theory has been reconfirmed by hobbyists in the United States and Europe.

Tortoise natural history indicates that hatchling Russian tortoises and Egyptian tortoises spend most of their early life hidden in moist soil, or in clumps of moist grass. Some species dwelling in the world's most arid deserts spend much of their lives in the bottoms of humid burrows. This humid microhabitat which hatchlings seek out is critical to prevention of pyramiding. In captivity, hobbyists often keep their tortoises in a dry environment, without the humid microclimate they experience in nature.

Slight pyramiding does not cause any health issues or affect the tortoise's ability to reproduce, but esthetically a smooth shell is preferred and is more natural.

Irregular Scutes

Tortoises are occasionally seen with irregular scutes in the form of an extra scute or a split scute. This condition is seen in captive-hatched specimens but does occur in nature as well.

The main cause of irregular scutes in captivity is incubation temperatures that are too high. High temperatures maintained to produce females or to accelerate hatching (or incubation accidents) may cause irregular scutes or other deformities. The control of incubation temperatures is critical as extreme incubation temperature will cause significant deformities or death.

These irregular scutes do not have an effect on the health of the tortoise and appear more prevalent in females. For this reason many tortoise breeders while searching through tortoises at reptile shows may look for tortoises with split scutes in hopes of finding a young female.

Chapter SEVEN: Breeding

Male Russian tortoises are very active breeders during much of the year. Photo by Jerry Fife.

Russian tortoises are sexually mature at about 4 inches (10 cm) for males and 7 inches (18 cm) for females. This is usually at four to seven years old, depending on the care they are receiving. Males mature at a smaller size than females.

The sex of a Russian tortoise is best determined by tail size. Males have a longer and thicker tail than females. Males do not have the concave plastron seen in males of many other tortoise species. Another determining factor is the configuration of the anal scutes. In males, the anal scutes are more elongated and have a wide angle of separation (for positioning their tail for breeding). In females, the anal scutes are less elongated and are directed toward the rear of the shell. This difference can be seen in young tortoises but doesn't necessarily persist as the tortoise grows so cannot be an indicator of sex in hatchlings.

A male Russian tortoise, *Agrionemys horsfieldii*. Photo by Jerry Fife.

Adult size and tail length and shape are the best indicators of sex.

Sexing

Sexing of young Russian tortoises may be difficult. Russian tortoises, as you will see in the previous photographs, are best sexed based on tail length, tail thickness, and configuration of the anal scutes. In Mediterranean tortoises such Hermann's, Egyptian, and Greek species, females are larger than males.

Courtship

Mating and courtship can be observed most frequently in spring and during periods without extreme temperatures. During summer on rainy and overcast days, all activity increases, including breeding. Nesting generally takes place in the spring from about February through June depending on temperatures. Once temperatures reach daily highs in the 70's F egg laying will begin, even though nighttime temperatures may still drop down into the 50's F. In Phoenix, Russian tortoises begin laying by March.

Reports of egg-laying almost year-round have been reported by some hobbyists keeping their tortoises indoors at optimal temperatures. Both extreme heat and cold seem to trigger a stop in reproduc-

A male's aggressive approach to a female. Photo by Jerry Fife.

Two Russian tortoise females laying eggs on a sunny April afternoon in Oklahoma. Photo by Jeff Littlejohn.

tion. In outdoor pens in Phoenix we also experience egg laying in the fall, once temperatures begin to cool down from the extreme heat of the summer.

Egg-Laying

The breeding and laying season depends on various factors, including the length of hibernation, climate, temperatures, health of the tortoises, and other factors. It is my opinion that the temperature is more critical than the length of daylight for reproduction cycles, however for indoor enclosures a 12-14 hour light cycle is recommended during periods of activity.

Russian tortoises typically produce two or three clutches of eggs from late March to mid-June, often at intervals of 16-18 days.

Often the female Russian tortoise will begin nesting in the morning or late afternoon before temperatures are too hot. The female will excavate a small hole and then wet the bottom of the hole with water from her urinary bladder. This water softens the bottom of the hole, which allows the female to then "flask out" or enlarge the bottom of the hole. This creates a small opening at ground level and a larger cavity below the ground that will accept the eggs. She will then begin laying eggs, one at a time. The eggs slowly slide down a mucus sleeve to the bottom of the nest cavity. It is important that the female be well-hydrated during this time so she can produce enough water to wet the bottom of the hole to excavate the nest cavity and to produce the mucus sleeve.

It is also important that the soil not contain large rocks as this will prevent the female from excavating her nest or result in broken eggs as they drop to the bottom of the nest. It is not unusual for a female to dig several test holes over a period of several days as she searches for just the right site with the proper conditions.

Once the eggs have been deposited, she will begin filling the nest cavity. Prior to filling the nest, the eggs may be removed by the keeper for incubation. The female should then be returned to the nest where she will continue to refill the empty hole. She will push the dirt into the hole and will firmly pack the surface of the nest with her hind feet and finally smooth it out, thereby hiding the nest. This entire process may take a couple of hours.

I have had Russian tortoises hatch naturally out of the ground in Phoenix, Arizona.

One of the first things anyone keeping mature Russian tortoises will quickly find out is how persistent and aggressive these species can be during courtship and mating. Leg biting, ramming and constant chasing are common. Each species may exhibit slightly different breeding tendencies, however all must be observed to ensure the safety of the female.

Russian tortoises, while being aggressive breeders, seldom display the level of leg biting and ramming of the other *Testudo*, however this is not always the case.

A hiding Russian tortoise may be escaping problems, especially if it hides during its usual active times. Photo by Chris Roscher.

The aggressive behavior of Russian tortoises may be addressed in several ways.

Separation

Except for breeding introductions in the spring and/or fall, males and females can be separated. This saves the female from constant torment and potentially fatal aggression from males. Some breeders believe that this also may increase the fertility of males resulting in improved hatch rates.

Multiple Females

Having multiple females may help reduce the stress on a single female, however females must still be monitored. This may also impact fertility (lower it) as the male's breeding frequency may not allow adequate recovery periods between mating.

Russian tortoise enclosure that features many sight barriers, resting areas, and natural and manmade shelters. Photo by Jerry Fife.

Enclosure Size & Setup

A large enclosure with a number of sight barriers and hide areas will allow multiple males and females to be kept together. It is still important to inspect females and be prepared to move a specimen if it is being harrassed or has been injured from courtship and breeding activity.

Chapter EIGHT: Eggs and Incubation

Russian tortoise hatching. Photo by Jerry Fife.

The goal of many hobbyists is to breed their tortoises; others simply find eggs in an enclosure and wonder what to do.

Once your tortoise digs a nest and lays eggs, what do you do next? There are two options:

Leave the eggs to hatch naturally out of the ground or dig them up to artificially incubate them.

If you live in a climate similar to their native range and have an area free of predators, tortoises will successfully hatch out of the ground. This, however, can be quite risky as rainfall may vary, temperatures may fluctuate, and hatchlings may fall prey to birds or other predators. Due to the many risks of leaving the eggs in the ground, I recommend that tortoise eggs be dug up and incubated. Artificial incubation also allows the keeper to better control the sex of the hatchlings as Russian tortoises are temperature sex determinant

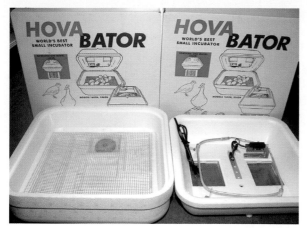

Inexpensive incubators can be used to successfully incubate tortoise eggs.

(TSD). The pivotal temperature where an equal number of males and females will be produced varies slightly with species but is around 87° F (30° C). Eggs incubated above these temperatures result in a higher degree of females and below in a higher percentage of males.

It is recommended that the eggs be removed before the female's backfilling operation begins or as the eggs are deposited. Once eggs are laid, they may be placed in a plastic shoebox containing two parts perlite to one part water by weight, and then incubated. The incubation medium should be damp but not wet, often perlite fresh from a sealed bag will have sufficient moisture, without the need for additional water.

I have had eggs break as they drop from the female and hit another egg or when the female begins covering and packing the nest with dirt. If eggs are removed before the female covers the eggs, the female is returned to the nest hole and she is allowed to complete the task of covering and filling an empty nest hole. When laid, the eggs are naturally coated with a thin layer of mucous that has antibacterial properties. Many hobbyists choose to wash eggs, however this removes the protective coating and I don't recommend it.

Incubation

A variety of incubation mediums may be used. Substrates may include: fine gravel, sand, soil, vermiculite, perlite, peat moss, and other materials. Each substrate has its own benefits. Some materials hold water, others allow better air circulation and gas exchange, but each has been successfully used. I generally prefer perlite, which allows proper air exchange and I like its ability to maintain adequate moisture levels.

Hatch-Rite™ is an excellent incubation medium used by many tortoise breeders.

The moisture level of the incubation substrate, humidity, and temperature all impact incubation periods. High temperatures and high humidity frequently cause premature hatching. Moisture levels that are too high will cause the eggs to crack, killing the embryo, or may result in premature hatchlings with large yolk sacs. Russian tortoises are less tolerant of extreme levels of moisture or humidity above 90% during incubation. The recommended level of humidity is 60%-80% relative humidity. The higher level of humidity should be associated with higher temperatures. If incubating at lower temperatures, the humidity should be maintained at the lower end of the range.

Incubation at constant temperatures may range between 77 to 90° F (25 to 32° C).

A recent hatchling tortoise with an umbilical "button". This area will heal up over the few days after hatching.

A Golden Greek tortoise (left) and a very dark Russian tortoise (right), soon after hatching. Photo by Jerry Fife.

Embryonic survival is impossible above 95° F (35° C). Constant incubation temperatures below 77° F (25° C) likewise will result in non-viable embryos. Higher and lower values are tolerated without lasting effects during incubation, if limited to brief periods of time (Diaz-Paniagua, 2006).

One of the advantages of keeping and breeding Mediterranean tortoises is that eggs hatch quickly and do not require unusual incubation techniques.

Incubation of Russian tortoise eggs may take 45 to 100 days, depending on the incubation temperatures. They typically hatch in about 60 days. Eggs from a single clutch generally hatch within a few days of each other, however on occasion it may take an extended period for all the eggs in a clutch to hatch.

It is important that the humidity level in the incubator be maintained above 60%. If the humidity level is too low the baby tortoise will not be able to escape from its shell.

Incubation medium that is too dry or a lack of humidity may kill the tortoise. It may seem that one would want to err on being too wet, but this is not the case.

Substrate that is too damp will cause the egg to absorb too much moisture causing it to split and rot. A slightly dry incubation medium, with high humidity in the incubator itself is better than an incubation medium that is too damp.

High incubation temperatures for tortoises often result in a high percentage of shell deformities such as extra scutes, split scutes or irregular shaped scutes. These deformities are generally not genetic and do not affect the health of the tortoise.

The excitement of seeing a small hatchling tortoise escape from the egg and then thrive under watchful care is something that never gets old. Hopefully, captive-hatched tortoises will someday make it unnecessary to remove tortoises from the wild. That is the hope of myself and most tortoise breeders around the world. Thank you for supporting their work.

PHOTO GALLERY

An adult Greek tortoise, *Testudo graeca graeca*, found in nature in Sardinia. Photo by Wolfgang Wegehaupt.

A Hermann's tortoise, *Testudo hermanni boettgeri*, photographed in Greece by Wofgang Wegehaupt.

A beautiful Golden Greek tortoise, *Testudo graeca terrestris*. Photo by Jerry Fife.

The striking Libyan Greek tortoise, *Testudo graeca cyrenaica*. Photo by Jerry Fife.

Testudo h. hermanni from Sardinia, laying eggs. Photo by Wolfgang Wegehaupt.

A hatchling Hermann's tortoise, *Testudo h. boettgeri* discovered in nature in Montenegro. Photo by Mario Schweiger.

Glossary

Amelanistic: Lacking melanin or black pigment.

Aestivation: The lowering of metabolic rate during hot periods or droughts.

Bask: To lie in a warm area, as under a heat lamp or in the sun, in order to absorb heat.

Binomial: A scientific name comprised of two parts, genus and species. Example: Pyxis arachnoides. Pyxis is the genus for the tortoise and arachnoides is the species name for the Spider tortoise.

Biology: The study of life and all life forms.

Brumation: Is the term for the hibernation like state that cold blooded reptiles use during very cold periods."Cooling" a herp by lowering its temperature for usually 2 to 4 months to approximate conditions during the winter period. Brumation triggers the physical changes that stimulate egg production in females, sperm production in males and the breeding response necessary for successful captive propagation.

Burrow: To dig underground for shelter or for the purpose of concealment. The tunnel created by a burrowing animal.

Carapace: A turtle or tortoise's upper shell.

CITES: Convention on International Trade in Endangered Species of wild flora and fauna. Entered into force in 1975, CITES is an international agreement designed to control the international trade in protected species of plants and animals. Participation of individual countries is voluntary.

Cloaca: The common terminal chamber for the intestinal and urogenital systems. Urinary and intestinal wastes collect here before passing out of the body. Eggs pass out of the oviduct through the cloaca when being laid. The cloaca terminates at an opening named the vent.

Clutch: A group of eggs laid by a reptile or bird.

Costal Scute: The scales/scutes along the sides of the carapace of a turtle or tortoise.

Dimorphism: Having two forms. Sexual dimorphism means that the females and males are different in appearance. Dimorphism is a special case of polymorphism, in which a species has more than one form.

Diurnal: Active during the day.

Ectoparasite: Parasites that affect an animal externally by attaching themselves to the skin and sucking blood from the host animal. Mites and ticks are ectoparasites in reptiles.

Ectotherm: An animal that cannot regulate its body temperature by an internal mechanism. Reptiles and amphibians are ectotherms. A "cold blooded" animal. Ectotherms regulate their body temperature by utilizing warm and cool zones in their environment.

Eggbound: A life-threatening condition that prevents a female reptile from laying her eggs. It may be caused by one or more (usually infertile) eggs adhering to the lining of the oviduct.

Endangered Species: An animal that is considered in danger of extinction. An animal or plant identified by a state, federal or other jurisdiction as being endangered.

Endangered Species Act of 1973: A US Federal Law that was passed for the purpose of protecting endangered and threatened species of flora and fauna. The Radiated and Galapagos tortoises are both listed on the US Endangered Species list, requiring federal permits for transferring across state lines.

Endemic species: A species native to a particular region.

Endoparasite: Parasites of the circulatory, digestive or pulmonary systems of reptiles. These include a variety of round worms, tapeworms, flukes, and protozoans.

Extinct: A species in which all living specimens have died. A species that no longer lives on earth.

Extirpate, Extirpated: A species that has been eliminated or no longer exists in a particular area where it was formerly found.

Gestation: The development of an embryo inside a female animal until it is fully developed and ready for birth. Gestation period: The period of egg development while the egg is still inside the female, before laying. The period of time it takes for an embryo to fully develop inside the female in live-bearing animals.

Gravid: A term used to describe a female reptile which is carrying eggs or young.

Herp: A slang term for any and all species of reptile and amphibian.

Herper: A slang term for a person who keeps, breeds, or collects reptiles or amphibians.

Herpetoculturist: 1. A person who breeds reptiles or amphibians. 2. A person who keeps or has a serious interest in reptiles or amphibians and is an active participant in the community of herpetoculture through involvement and participation in clubs and organizations, shows, lectures and symposia, or online in message boards and chat rooms.

Herpetologist: A person who studies reptiles and amphibians. There is no specific degree in Herpetology in the United States, so a Herpetologist will usually have a degree in Biology and Zoology, with graduate work in the discipline of Herpetology.

Herbivorous, Herbivore: An animal that eats vegetation or plant matter.

Husbandry: The different aspects and techniques of caring for an animal.

Impaction: A condition where a looped intestine or a plug of some foreign matter makes the animal unable to pass waste material through the intestine to the outside. This is often a fatal condition. Tortoises which ingest sand or rocks may become impacted. An impaction may also be the result of egg retention.

Incubate: To maintain eggs in conditions favorable to development and hatching.

Incubator: A device used to incubate eggs.

Melanistic: Having an excess of melanin or black pigment.

Metabolic Bone Disease: A disease commonly seen in lizards and turtles that affects bone development resulting in malformed bones. It is normally caused by dietary or vitamin deficiencies such as the lack of usable calcium.

Neonate: A newly hatched or newborn animal.

Nocturnal: Active at night.

Nuchal scute: The scutes, or scales, on a tortoise or turtle's carapace located above the neck.

Omnivorous, Omnivore: An animal that eats both plant and animal matter.

Oviparous: Egg laying.

Pip: The act, by a baby reptile or bird, of cutting its way out of the egg using a special egg tooth or caruncle.

Plastron: The bottom shell of a turtle or tortoise.

Scute: An enlarged scale, or the outer plate on the shell of a turtle or tortoise.

Scientific Name: Scientific names are made up of the genus, species and subspecies (if applicable) names. For example, the scientific name of a Spider Tortoise would be *Pyxis arachnoide brygooi*. You will frequently see this abbreviated as *P. a. brygooi* AFTER the full species name has been mentioned in whatever text you are reading. Scientific names should be in italics or underlined if italics are not possible to print. Only the genus name is capitalized.

Spur: A small appendage typically located on the hind legs or tip of the tail in tortoises. This spur results in one of the common names for Greek tortoises – Spur Thighed Tortoise. (Other species, such as the African Spurred Tortoise also have spurs on their hind legs.)

Stomatitis: An infection of the lining of a reptile's mouth. It is usually caused by bacteria and is characterized by a cheesy discharge from the lesions and unwillingness to feed. Severe cases can cause death.

Subadult: A juvenile animal that is nearing sexual maturity.

Subspecies: A taxonomic division of a species into geographic races.

Substrate: Material used to cover the bottom of a cage. Newspaper, bark chips, mulch, peat moss, grass clippings, dirt and sand are forms of substrates.

Taxonomy: The systematic naming of animals and plants. The scientific name of a plant or an animal.

Terrestrial: Living on the ground. An animal that spends most of its time on the ground.

Thermal gradient: A gradual change in temperature from one part of a cage to another.

Thermoregulation: Moving from a warm area to a cooler one or vice-versa in order to regulate body temperature in cold blooded reptiles.

Threatened: A species that is not yet endangered, but is in danger of becoming endangered. An official designation by regulatory body or agency indicating that a species may be in need of protection or regulation due to its status in the wild.

Trio: Refers to a breeding group, usually 1 male and 2 females.

Vent: The opening at the end of the cloaca (see Cloaca) where urinary waste, intestinal waste, and eggs leave a tortoise's body.

Conversion Chart

Length

1 Centimeter (cm) = .39 Inches   1 Inch = 2.54 Centimeters
1 Meter (m) = 3.28 Feet   1 Foot = .3 Meters
1 Meter = 1.09 Yards   1 Yard = .9 Meters
1 Kilometer (km) = .62 Miles   1 Mile = 1.6 Kilometers

Area

1 Hectare (ha) = 2.472 Acres   1 Acre = .4 Hectares
1 Hectare = 1,000 Square Meters   1 Acre = 4840 Square Yards

Weights

1 Milligram (mg) = .001 Grams
1 Gram (g) = .035 Ounce   1 Ounce (oz) = 28.3 Grams
1 Kilogram (kg) = 2.2 Pounds   1 Pound (lb) = .45 Kilograms

Temperature Conversion

Fahrenheit to Celsius = F - 32 x 5/9
Celsius to Fahrenheit = C x 9/5) + 32

SUGGESTED READING

Anderson, S. C. 1963. Amphibians and Reptiles from Iran. Proc. Calif.
Acad. Sci. 4th series, 31:417-498.

Das, I. 1995. Turtles and tortoises of India. Oxford Univ. Press, Bombay.
179 pp.

Domenge, Alain. 2003. *Agrionemys horsfieldii* (ou *Testudo horsfeldii*), la
Tortue des steppes. Manouria. 6(20):5-12.

Ernst,C.H. and R. W. Barbour. 1989. Turtles of the World. Smithsonian
Institution Press, Washington D.C. - London.

Fife, J. 2012. MEDITERRANEAN TORTOISES: The Natural History,
Captive Care, and Breeding of Greeks, Hermann's, Marginated, Russian,
and Egyptian Tortoises. Living Art publishing, Ada, Oklahoma.

Gurley, R. 2006. Sulcatas in Captivity (With Notes on Other Popular Tortoises). ECO publishing. Portal, New Mexico.

Highfield, A. C. 2000. The Tortoise and Turtle Feeding Manual. Carapace
Press. UK.

Highfield, A. C. 1996. The Practical Encyclopedia of Keeping and Breeding Tortoises and Freshwater Turtles. Carapace Press. UK.

Kami, H. G.. 1999. On the biology of the Afghan Tortoise, *Testudo hors-
fieldi*, in north-eastern Iran (Reptilia: Testudines). Zoology in the Middle
East 19: 43.

Lagarde, F., X. Bonnet and R. Bour. 2004. *Agrionemys horsfieldii*. Manouria. 7 (22):47-49.

Pirog, E. 2005. Russian Tortoises. Complete Herp Care Series. TFH Publications, Inc. Neptune, NJ.

Pritchard, P. 1979. Encyclopedia of Turtles. TFH Publications, Inc. Neptune, NJ.

Vetter, H. 2006. Turtles of the World, vol 4: East and South Asia. Edition
Chimaira, Germany.

ABOUT THE AUTHOR

The author at his home in Arizona. Photo by Richard Fife.

Jerry Fife is a former CPA who has managed golf courses, sports complexes, and the spring training baseball stadiums and practice facilities for the Oakland A's and Milwaukee Brewers. He has bred tortoises and lizards for over a decade. He currently works with all of the Mediterranean tortoise species and has bred Greeks, Hermann's, Marginateds, Russian, and Egyptian tortoises. He has produced hatchlings of all five species both indoors using artificial incubation and out of the ground in his outdoor enclosures.

Jerry travels frequently and has recently visited the Caribbean, Mexico, Galapagos Islands, Fiji, and Central America. He is the author of *A Pictorial Guide to Iguanas of the World*, *Leopard Tortoises: The Natural History, Captive Care and Breeding of Stigmochelys pardalis* (with his brother, Richard Fife), *Star Tortoises: The Natural History, Captive Care, and Breeding of Geochelone elegans and Geochelone platynota*, and *Mediterranean Tortoises: Natural History, Captive Care, and Breeding of Greek, Hermann's, Marginated, Russian & Egyptian Tortoises*.